D0819602

Published by Creative Education
123 South Broad Street, Mankato, Minnesota 56001
Creative Education is an imprint of The Creative Company

Designed by Stephanie Blumenthal

Photographs by Richard Cummins, Victor Englebert, Image Finders (Bachman, Eric Berndt, Mark Gibson,
Jeff Greenberg), Gunter Marx, Robert McCaw, Paul McMahon, Karlene Schwartz, Tom Stack & Associates (Bob Pool,
Milton Rand, Inga Spence, John Shaw, Greg Vaughn), Doug Wilson, Unicorn Stock Photos (B. W. Hoffman,
Frank Pennington, Jim Shippee)

Copyright © 2002 Creative Education.
International copyrights reserved in all countries.
No part of this book may be reproduced in any form without
written permission from the publisher.

Library of Congress Cataloging-in-Publication Data

Hurwitz, Ellen.
Grains / by Ellen Hurwitz and Scott Wrobel.
p. cm. — (Let's investigate)
Includes index.
ISBN 0-88682-970-4
1. Grain—Juvenile literature. [1. Grain.] I. Wrobel, Scott. II. Title.
III. Let's investigate (Mankato, Minn.)
SB189 .H97   2001
633.1—dc21   00-047389

First edition

2 4 6 8 9 7 5 3 1

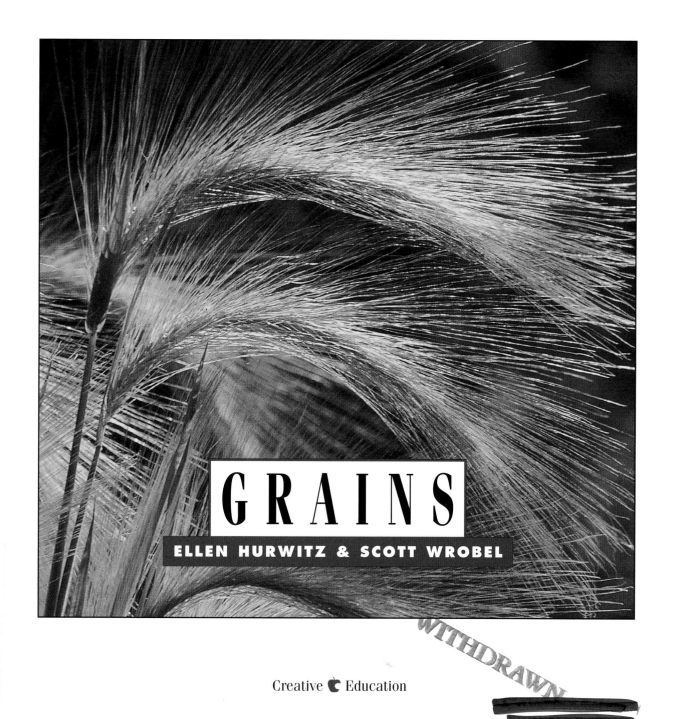

GRAINS

ELLEN HURWITZ & SCOTT WROBEL

Creative Education

T 39597

WITHDRAWN

GRAINS

STRAW

Some of the very first papers were made from grain straw. If wood pulp was not available, wheat straw could be used to make newspapers, cardboard, and office paper.

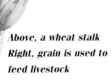

Above, a wheat stalk Right, grain is used to feed livestock

Grain is one of the world's most important crops. We use it to make everyday foods, such as bread, cooking oil, and cereal, and many things that aren't food, such as paper, starch, and glue. Even when people think they're eating something else—when they drink milk or eat meat, eggs, or cheese—they're eating grain indirectly, because the animals that produced those products were fed grain. Grain keeps us all alive.

GRAINS
FAMILY

Members of the grass family grow in deserts, in water, and even in polar regions. They range in height from one inch (2.5 cm) to 100 feet (30.5 m) tall.

Right, wild grasses on the prairie
Below, bundled bamboo

Grain comes from plants that are members of the grass family. This is a huge family. It has more than 5,000 members, ranging from bamboo and sugar cane to the smaller, softer grasses that cows, sheep, and horses eat.

All the grains grown in the world today were first cultivated by our Stone Age ancestors. Later humans developed new varieties of these early grains, but we haven't discovered any grains that weren't known in the Stone Age.

7

Before prehistoric humans learned to grow grain, they gathered the seeds of wild grasses and ate them. These people moved from place to place, looking for wild plants to gather and for animals to hunt. Eventually, they learned to **cultivate** the grasses, and this changed the way they lived. They could stop moving from place to place. In time, they grew more food than they could eat themselves, so some people could stop farming and do other kinds of work. They began to trade the things they made and the food they raised with other people. They built the first towns, and later they built cities.

All early civilizations developed out of the cultivation of grain. Even today, grain is the most important food in the diet of many of the world's people.

Above, the South American grain quinoa Left, wild grass was an important food source for early humans

GRAINS

PROTEIN

Meat, cheese, milk, and fish are all complete proteins, but humans can also get complete proteins by combining grains with beans, nuts, and vegetables.

GRAINS

BRAN

Brown rice is rice with the bran layer and germ left on. White rice is rice without the bran and germ. Brown rice is a better source of nutrition than white rice but it spoils more quickly.

Corn on the cob is a sweet-tasting corn

GRAIN AS FOOD

Relative to the time humans put into growing them, grains give us more food value than any other crop. They're rich in carbohydrates (car-bo-HY-drates), which the body needs for energy. The body also needs protein (PRO-teen) and fat, and grains give us some of these.

rotein is particularly complicated because it's made up of 20 amino (ah-MEE-no) acids. The human body can make 11 of these by itself, but it has to get the other nine from food. People who don't get all nine amino acids from their food will have less energy and less resistance to disease than people with better diets. Children who don't eat all nine amino acids can become seriously ill or even die as a result.

GRAINS
POPCORN

When a kernel of popcorn is heated, steam builds up inside the shell until it explodes. Only hard corn can be used for popcorn. Soft corn won't pop.

Above, popcorn kernels

GRAINS
RICE

Most rice is eaten in the country that grows it. Less than five percent of the world's rice is shipped from one country to another.

*Above, cooked rice
Right, large fields
of rice*

Foods that supply all nine amino acids are called complete proteins. Foods that supply only some of the nine are called incomplete proteins. But incomplete proteins can be eaten together to make a complete protein. No type of grain is a complete protein, but some grains come closer than others.

Many people prefer to eat grains such as rice and wheat only after the bran layers and the germ are removed. Bran is a tough coating around the endosperm, or starchy center of the grain, and it contains many vitamins and minerals. The germ is the small part of the **kernel** from which a new plant would sprout. Once the bran is stripped away, what's left is not as **nutritious** as the whole grain, so vitamins are sometimes added to replace the nutrition lost in processing.

GRAINS
RICE

In poorer countries, where labor is plentiful and machinery is expensive, rice is planted, harvested, and threshed by hand. In industrialized countries, machinery is used.

Above, workers tend rice fields by hand in many countries

GRAINS

In the industrialized world, grain is often used to feed both animals and people. In poorer countries, people can't afford to feed grain to animals. They eat more grain and less meat than people in richer countries.

12

FROM GRAIN TO FLOUR

Much of the grain grown in the world today is eaten whole, either by livestock or by humans, but a lot of it is ground into flour and then made into breads and other baked goods. Humans have made grain into flour for thousands of years. The earliest way of making flour was to pour the grain onto a rock that was shaped like a saddle or a bowl and then grind it with another rock. This worked, but it took a lot of time and work to produce just a little bit of flour.

Sacks of flour

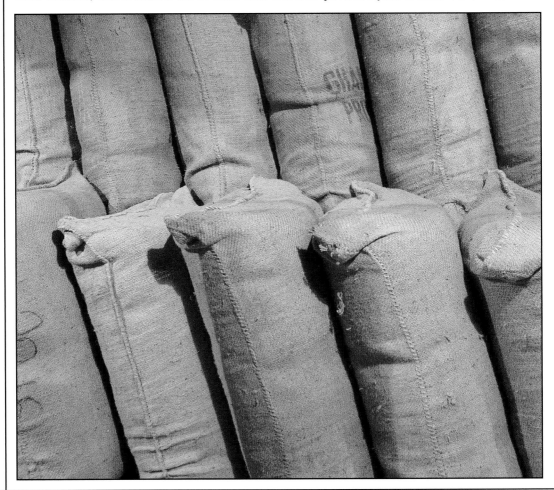

Millstones changed that. People discovered that they could make high-quality flour by placing the grain on one large stone and then spinning another stone on top of the grain. The top stone had to be heavy, so many of the first flour mills used large animals, such as oxen, for power. The animal would walk in a circle, pushing or pulling a pole that was attached to the top stone. This turned the stone, which ground the grain into flour as it spun.

GRAINS

TAXES

Grain was such an important part of life in ancient Egypt, Greece, and Rome that people often used it as payment for their taxes.

Above, bundled wheat Left, oxen were often used to power early flour mills

GRAINS

*Grain confusion:
Grain plants are
sometimes called
cereals, or cereal
grains. The seeds of
grain plants are also
called grain.*

14

**An old-fashioned
flour mill**

Later, people found that they could use wind and water to turn their mills more quickly. Today, in the world's industrialized countries, big machines grind the grain. A modern flour mill can turn four million pounds (1.8 million kg) of wheat into three million pounds (1.35 million kg) of flour in one day.

GRAINS
CEREALS

Ready-to-eat cereals were first introduced at the end of the 19th century. Before that, all cereals had to be cooked.

An old windmill in a field of golden wheat

GRAINS

PLANTING

In China, many farmers plant corn, cotton, or soybeans between their rows of wheat.

Above, wheat stalks
Right, vast wheat fields
in the northwestern
United States

WHEAT

People grow more wheat than any other grain, and wheat covers more land than any other food crop. It was probably first cultivated around 9000 B.C. in the Middle East. By 4000 B.C., its cultivation had spread to much of Asia, Europe, and North Africa. It was brought to the Americas by European explorers.

GRAINS

USAGE

Hard wheat is used for bread, macaroni, spaghetti, and other pastas. Soft wheat is used to make pastries, such as cakes and cookies.

GRAINS

WINTER

Winter wheat is planted in the fall and harvested in the spring or summer. It stops growing over the winter, but it won't produce a crop unless it is exposed to cold weather.

Wheat is used to make bread and many other foods

Wheat is a good source of protein, and people eat it in breakfast cereals, breads, crackers, cakes, cookies, noodles, and many other common foods. The bran and germ that are removed from wheat to make white flour can be fed to livestock, but they are such good sources of vitamins, minerals, and fiber that some people buy them separately to add to their food.

Although it often goes to waste in industrialized countries, wheat **straw** can be used in many ways. It can be braided into baskets and hats or used on fields for fertilizer. It can also be used to make paper and livestock bedding. Glues from wheat starch are so strong that they are used to hold the layers of plywood together.

Spring wheat is planted in the spring and harvested in the summer. It doesn't produce as rich a crop as winter wheat, but it will grow where the climate is too cold for winter wheat.

19

*Above, wheat kernels
Left, a grain elevator in
a field of cut wheat*

GRAINS
D I E T

*Half the **calories** in the diet of many people in Asia come from rice.*

Right, rice farms are common throughout much of China
Below, rice plant shoots

RICE

Rice is the most important food for more than half the people in the world. No one knows exactly when or where it originated, but by 5000 B.C. rice was being grown in what is now southern China and in parts of Southeast Asia. From there, it spread throughout Asia and into the Middle East. The Moors brought rice to Europe from northwest Africa in the 700s, and Europeans brought it to the Americas.

Even though protein makes up only a small part of the rice kernel, rice is a good source of protein if people eat enough of it. Most rice is boiled and eaten whole, but it can also be ground into flour, **fermented** into wine or beer, or used in breakfast cereals, soups, baby foods, and snack foods.

GRAINS

NUTRITIONAL

There are millions of "subsistence farms" in the world. Each of these farms grows only enough food to feed the family that lives and works on it.

Above, cabbage and rice grow in similar conditions

GRAINS

INEDIBLE

Parts of the rice plant can be used in livestock feed, packing, insulation, bricks, cement, soaps, paper, plastics, shatterproof glass, buttons, sausage, fertilizer, and other products.

Above, rice seedlings ready for planting Right, growing rice seed heads

lmost all parts of the rice plant can be used. Rice hulls, the **inedible** covering of the kernel, can be used in insulation and cement. The straw can be used to **thatch** roofs, or it can be woven into sandals, hats, and baskets. It can also be made into high-quality paper.

GRAINS

MAIZE

Corn is also called maize. Humans probably first used it for food around 8000 B.C. in what is now Mexico. At first, people gathered corn as a wild grain. Then, around 5000 B.C., they started to cultivate it, passing along what they learned to people throughout South, Central, and North America. When Europeans first came to the Americas, they learned from the Native Americans how to grow and use corn. The explorer Christopher Columbus brought some back to Spain. Within one generation, corn had spread throughout Europe. Within two generations, it had reached Africa and Asia. Today, corn is grown in the Americas, Africa, Asia, southern Europe, and the Middle East—wherever in the world the climate allows.

More grain confusion: In England and Europe, the word "corn" refers to any grain used to make bread. In America, it means one particular kind of grain: maize.

A young husk of corn

C orn is not a complete protein, so Native Americans combined it with beans and squash, which complete the protein. When corn alone is people's main food, as it is in some parts of the **developing world**, the people are likely to suffer from **malnutrition**.

Corn is often eaten boiled, but it is also used to make breakfast cereals, tortillas, hominy, corn bread, snack foods, salad dressings, margarine, whiskey, and sweeteners. It is also fed to livestock and can be used to make ceramics, explosives, construction materials, paint, paper goods, penicillin, and cloth.

Native Americans used corn to make foods, medicines, scrub brushes, baskets, dolls, wrappings, flour, alcohol, sweeteners, and many other things.

Corn is a popular grain grown in many parts of the world

GRAINS

GODDESS

The word "cereal" comes from Ceres (SIHR-eez), the name of the Roman goddess of farming. Pictures of Ceres often show her with ears of barley braided into her hair.

Barley is used to make cereals, malt beverages, and livestock feed

OTHER GRAINS

Barley may have been the first grain ever eaten by humans. It was grown by the ancient Chinese, Greeks, and Romans, and it has been found at a Stone Age site in what is now Switzerland. Barley is the **hardiest** of the grains, and it grows best in cool climates. Today, it is fed to livestock and eaten by humans in soups, breads, and baby foods. It can also be made into malt, which is used to make beer, liquor, and malted milk.

Grain sorghum is only one variety of sorghum. The other sorghums are sweet sorghum, grassy sorghum, and broom corn. Sorghums can be made into sweeteners, waxes, malt, beer, brooms, starch, and livestock feed.

.

27

Grain sorghum was probably first cultivated in Africa. It was brought to North America in the 1800s. In Africa and Asia, grain sorghum seeds are often ground into flour for breads, cakes, or **porridge**, or roasted and eaten whole. The stalks can be fed to animals or used as building material. In North America, sorghum is grown mostly for animal feed. It is prized in hot, dry climates because it resists heat and **drought**.

Above, sorghum seeds Left, sorghum crops are often harvested using combines

GRAINS

Rye can grow in colder climates than wheat. It grows as far north as the Arctic Circle.

Above, oat seeds Right, a ripening oat plant

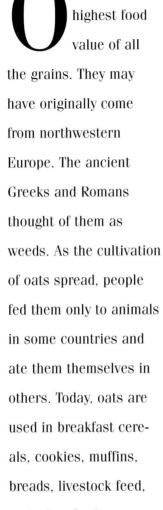

Oats have the highest food value of all the grains. They may have originally come from northwestern Europe. The ancient Greeks and Romans thought of them as weeds. As the cultivation of oats spread, people fed them only to animals in some countries and ate them themselves in others. Today, oats are used in breakfast cereals, cookies, muffins, breads, livestock feed, and other foods.

Rye is grown mostly to feed people, and it is almost as nutritious as wheat. It is used to make bread and liquor, and the straw is used for packing material, paper, mats, roof thatch, and hats. Rye grows well in poor soil. It is also able to withstand cold climates better than most grains.

GRAINS

R Y E

Rye straw is so tough that not even cattle can eat it.

Above, rye straw can be used to thatch roofs Left, rye grass cut and ready to be harvested

GRAINS

WILD RICE

Wild rice has to be gathered before it's completely ripe or the grains will fall into the water at the slightest touch and be lost.

Above, unripened rice
Right, a quinoa field
Far right, mature rice seeds before harvest

Quinoa (KEEN-wah) is grain native to the Andes Mountains in South America. It was so important to the Incas that they called it "the mother grain." Quinoa can be cooked whole, like rice, or ground into flour for bread and tortillas, or popped like corn. The leaves can also be cooked and eaten like spinach or fed to livestock. Both the leaves and the seeds are good sources of protein.

Wild rice is a grain but not a close relative of cultivated rice. Wild rice is native to North America, China, and Japan. It grows wild in the shallow waters of marshes, lakes, and streams. This rice was an important food for Native Americans. Today, the truly wild variety is still harvested in some places, but it is also grown in paddies.

Grains were the foundation on which all the early civilizations were built. Even today, these ancient plants keep us all alive.

Glossary

Calories are a measure of the energy the human body gets from a particular food.

If people **cultivate** a plant, they plant it and take care of it.

The **developing world** is made up of poorer, less industrialized countries.

A **drought** is a long spell of dry weather.

When grain is **fermented**, the starch turns to alcohol.

The **hardiest** plants are those best able to survive in difficult weather conditions.

If something is **inedible**, it can't be eaten.

The **kernel** is the whole seed of a grain plant.

Malnutrition comes from not eating enough food, or from not eating enough different kinds of food.

A food that is **nutritious** is rich in some of the elements the body needs.

Porridge is a soft food made by boiling grain meal.

Once the grain has been removed, the stalk that the grain grew on is called **straw**.

To make a roof from plant material, such as straw, reeds, or large leaves, is to **thatch** a roof.

Index